What Our Readers Have Said...

"Although I consider myself a seasoned sales professional, it is helpful to have past learning's refreshed. The books were also beneficial because of the information concerning 'trends' in the sales relationship. The sales process should be viewed as dynamic since business relationships change regularly."

•

"For the particular business I am in and the type of sales calls I have, I find that the books in the Pinpoint Sales Training Series are very often applicable to how I conduct business. I would recommend them to other sales people, just not ones that are in my industry."

•

"These books provide very good concepts. It fits in well with the Bell Leadership training program that I attended in November."

•

"I use this material in these books and apply it to my customers and other employees I work with."

•

"I would like to know other topics. Is there anything on Production Management or Consultative Selling or Time Management?"

•

"These books are great tools that should be used as guidelines for our everyday

supervisory practices. You need to take the time to do a short self-evaluation when reading them."

•

"The Pinpoint Training Series delivers information that could be used in a lot different areas."

•

"I like this because I can take them with me to read at a convenient time. I feel the little time I have to spend in the office is best use on activities that directly relate to revenue opportunities. I like the short amount of time it takes to keep up with these."

•

"I prefer the self-study approach; it fits in with my schedule."

•

"My thought is that the real value of these books comes into effect when doing the action plans."

•

"Short and sweet. These books are easy to comprehend."

•

"I have enjoyed reading these books. They are relevant to today's work environment and the ongoing change in the way we manage our workforce."

•

"I do feel that these books have been very helpful to me at my job."

•

"I think a lot of the recommendations in these books are very useful, and can be applicable to everyday situations. If nothing else, it's a good reference guide to fall back upon if a situation arises in the future."

•

"These books are relevant to today's work environment and the ongoing change in the way we manage our workforce."

•

Closing More Sales

Pinpoint Sales Skill Development Training Series

TIMOTHY F. BEDNARZ

MAJORIUM
BUSINESS PRESS

Pinpoint Sales Skill Development Training Series
"Closing More Sales"
Timothy F. Bednarz

Graphic design: Monika Pawlak

Majorium Business Press
2025 Main Street
Stevens Point, WI 54481
715.342.1018 • 800.654.4935

ISBN 978-1-882181-63-6

Printed in the United States of America

Introduction

The Pinpoint Sales Skill Development Training Series is designed for targeted training and education regarding increased improvement in a specific skill or competency.

Each book within this series is designed to be easy to use, understand and apply to your job. It can be used as a basis for training individuals, as a discussion guide or as a personal training tool.

Each chapter within this book discusses a specific concept. When you have completed all eight chapters you should have a 360° perspective of the topic.

Additionally, each chapter is divided into specific sections:

- The first section provides you with an overview of the topic
- The Implications section discusses why the concept is important, and why it is important to learn and apply.
- The Strategies, Tips & Techniques to Apply section teaches how to use and apply the particular concept to your work.
- The Points to Ponder section gives you something to think about or to be discussed with a group setting. These are questions not meant to be immediately answered, but to be pondered over time.
- The Training Activity section provides you with the tools to transfer what you have learned to your job. It is designed to help create an action plan to effectively apply the concept.

Each of the topics in this series is time-tested and proven in the marketplace. They have been used by thousands of employees as training tools. Many of the users have commented that what made these books valuable, was the ability to refer to them when a problem surfaced. They indicated that they remembered reading about the exact problem. They referred back to these books and found an appropriate solution.

You will find them equally valuable as a resource in your professional development library.

Table of Contents

LEARNING OBJECTIVES:

- To determine if and when closing is a necessary skill to employ.
- To assist the prospect to buy.
- To gain a buyer's commitment.
- How to get the buyer to agree to the sale.
- To determine what to do if the buyer stalls.

1

Is It Necessary to Close the Sale?

Many salespeople have been trained in what is called the sales track style of selling, in which the salesperson presents a series of options to the buyer, overcomes objections and moves the buyer to a close. This style of selling, while still widespread, is no longer effective, as customers view it as manipulating them. Generally viewed negatively, the days when hard closes could be used effectively are long past.

IMPLICATIONS — WHAT THIS MEANS TO YOU

Today's buyers are more sophisticated than those in past decades. They are more educated and trained in obtaining the best values for their companies. Additionally, they are better versed in the myriad of buying options available to them. Skeptical of undocumented sales claims, they take the time to research their options, and are highly resistant to the manipulative pitches of the salesperson attempting to close the sale.

The salesperson who understands how today's buyer evaluates and purchases a product is able to use this knowledge to help them agree to the purchase. The salesperson who lacks this knowledge and relies instead on outmoded closing techniques places him or herself at a distinct competitive disadvantage.

STRATEGIES, TIPS & TECHNIQUES TO APPLY

The old approach to selling ends when the customer makes a purchase. The whole focus is on making the sale by presenting the customer with a series of options, one of which the salesperson hopes will fit a customer's requirements. They push through a process fraught with pitfalls and objections, ending with the salesperson sparring with the customer and then manipulating them into the sale. Once the salesperson makes the sale, he or she is off to the next customer.

This process fails to account for the fact that for the customer, the sale begins—not ends—when the order is placed and the product is delivered. Numerous surveys have indicated that one of the biggest customer fears is that the salesperson will disappear after the sale has been consummated.

The salesperson who is focused on the customer, approaches the sale from an entirely different perspective. They take the time to analyze the customer's business and explore their needs before they even begin to propose a solution. They carefully move the process forward until the sale is agreed upon. There is no need for a hard close. Typical objections are avoided because the salesperson carefully qualify

Most importantly, the sale itself is only one step in the process. The salesperson recognizes that value is delivered when the customer's expectations are repeatedly met. This means they are there when the product is delivered and installed. They are there when the customer's employees are taught how to use the product. And at whatever point they are needed, they are there to assure that the customer is satisfied.

The customer-focused salesperson is able to effectively build long-term relationships by continually delivering and assuring value to their customers. They understand that they are focused on meeting their customer's constantly changing concerns and needs.

A salesperson's motivation is transparent to the customer. If the salesperson is only motivated by commissions, the customer will recognize this. Salespeople are not selling in a void. Buyers are dealing with numerous salespeople from various vendors. They are able to recognize the salesperson who is genuinely concerned about their needs and interested in helping them obtain their goals and objectives.

POINTS TO PONDER — SOMETHING TO THINK ABOUT

1. What is your selling style? Do you feel it is effective?
2. How hard do you feel you need to close to get a sale?

TRAINING ACTIVITY — APPLICATION & ACTION PLAN

Examine your own selling style by considering the following points:

1. Where is your focus? Do you feel it is on the customer or on your own personal needs?
2. What is your goal? To make the sale and move on, or to assure the customer is satisfied with their purchase?
3. Where are you after the sale has been made? Are you moving on to the next customer or are you assuring that the customer and his or her employees know how best to use your product?
4. How do you think your customers perceive you as a salesperson?
5. What do you need to do to be more customer-focused?

2

Giving the Prospect a Reason to Buy

People buy on emotion and use facts to justify their decision. Manipulative sales techniques used over the years are met with resistance from today's buyers. They force the buyer into a decision they don't necessarily want to make and one that most likely doesn't appeal to their emotional needs. Effective salespeople don't sell, they help the customer to buy. The truth is people love to buy, but hate to be sold.

Customers are seeking solutions to their problems. The salesperson who is able to present the best available option to the customer will often get the sale. This means providing information and guidance that support customers' buying objectives.

IMPLICATIONS – WHAT THIS MEANS TO YOU

The salesperson who attempts to force the issue by selling his or her products with manipulative selling techniques is often viewed as pushy and obnoxious. Their personal focus on the sale is readily transparent. The sale to the buyer begins when he or she make the purchase, not when the salesperson concludes the sale.

One of the biggest customer fears is that the salesperson will flee once the sale is made. They want the salesperson to be as available after the sale as before to quickly resolve difficulties or problems. They want to deal with salespeople they can trust to stand behind their products and promises.

People buy from salespeople they like. Until a relationship of trust is firmly established, the sale will not be made. This is why it is essential to build rapport and establish a relationship where trust is built and solidified.

Without a relationship of trust, all the skills and talents a salesperson demonstrates will amount to nothing. When the customer trusts a salesperson, they will feel that he or she has placed their best interest ahead of the sale and will be open to their recommendations and suggestions.

STRATEGIES, TIPS & TECHNIQUES TO APPLY

Since the sale ultimately hinges on an emotional decision, salesmen and women must be aware of the perceptions and expectations they create with the customer. These perceptions and expectations will evolve as the customer is informed of all available options. The salesperson must be constantly attuned to these changes in the customer's thinking.

The customer's buying decision often hinges on a relatively small and easily overlooked product feature or detail. It is up to the salesperson to determine what is important to the customer, and create a desire in them for one or more differentiating features not found in the competitor's product or service.

The process of helping the customer to buy starts by identifying problems, needs and concerns that the buyer is seeking to resolve. This is accomplished through the use of open-ended questions that gently probe for information the salesperson can use to craft a buying solution. When customers feel they are being subjected to an interrogation, they immediately resist any inclination to provide the information needed to move the sales process forward. Thus, gathering information should be a comfortable discussion of the customer's needs and concerns guided by the salesperson's skillful use of these questions.

Another oft-overlooked pitfall lies in the fact that customers carefully evaluate salespeople according to their manner, demeanor and professionalism and how they handle themselves. The salesperson must be aware of this ongoing evaluation and be attuned to the nonverbal cues the customer may be sending. Posture, facial expressions, gestures, affectations—all are clear indicators of the emotional state of the customer and should guide the salesperson through a smooth and productive selling process.

POINTS TO PONDER — SOMETHING TO THINK ABOUT

1. How can you identify ways to make it easier for the customer to buy from you?
2. What techniques do you employ to uncover the needs and concerns a customer wishes to resolve? Explain.

TRAINING ACTIVITY — APPLICATION & ACTION PLAN

1. On a sheet of paper, create two columns and head them "Emotional Reasons" and "Facts."
2. In the first column list all of the emotional reasons why a customer might be motivated to buy your product or service. Across from each emotional reason, list a supporting fact.
3. Determine how you can trigger these emotional responses in your customers and then support them with the facts. Brainstorm with other salespeople to identify your customers' potential emotional hot buttons.

3

The Most Effective Closing Techniques

The vast majority of salespeople have been trained to sell using the sales track method, which builds the sale up to a point when the salesperson presses the customer to buy using manipulative selling techniques. They equate closing with asking for the order.

This method, still widely taught and practiced, is not only outmoded but also is resented by most customers who have firsthand experience with its effects.

IMPLICATIONS – WHAT THIS MEANS TO YOU

The problem with the sales track method of selling is that it focuses the salesperson on making the sale and attaining the subsequent commission check. It is a "selling at any cost" philosophy that has many customers wondering if the sale is being made at their expense.

No one wants to feel used or be manipulated solely for a salesperson's commission. This is one of the primary reasons that most customers are fearful the salesperson will quickly disappear after the sale has been culminated. They have repeatedly experienced this type of sale and are leery.

Salespeople do not sell in a void: all are affected by the sum total of experiences a customer has had with a host of other salespeople and techniques. This collective experience forms the basis of a skepticism and paranoia that result in objections, stalls and resistance to many salespeople, especially when they fail to build trust with the sales track method.

To avoid these problems, salespeople must employ sales techniques that recognize the unique needs of each customer and work with the customer to develop equally unique solutions.

STRATEGIES, TIPS & TECHNIQUES TO APPLY

No salesperson can be successful without the ability to ask for the order. However, there is no hard and fast rule that states that every sale must build up to a critical point where the salesperson must pose this specific question.

Another sales fallacy, especially in high-pressured selling environments is the "ABC – Always Be Closing" sales rule. This concept indicates the salesperson should always be pressing the customer for the sale. Typically this philosophy only serves to produce increased sales resistance.

However, viewed from a different perspective, the "Always Be Closing" rule makes a great deal of sense. Research indicates that the average sale takes eight sales calls while the majority of salespeople quit by the fifth. In the current economic environment, the sales cycle has lengthened appreciably.

With this in mind, the astute salesperson recognizes the various steps required for diagnosing, analyzing and identifying the customer's needs. In this regard, the salesperson uses the "Always Be Closing" philosophy not to close the sale, but to get the customer to agree to every aspect of the sale. It is easier to get a customer to agree to minor details than to agree to a major sale.

Salespeople who can get a customer to agree to a series of minor points and details along the way will find it relatively easy to get them to commit or agree to the sale. This technique paces the customer and leads them toward an agreement.

During every step of the sales process, the salesperson gets the customer to agree to the problem, need, solution or detail. The point is to get the customer to a continuous bridge of agreement. At the beginning of every contact, the salesperson reviews the key points of agreement. At the conclusion, they also review the points the customer just agreed to. The logical conclusion of this process is that the customer ultimately agrees to the sale.

It should be noted that this technique does not manipulate or compel a customer to buy, but builds the sale one step at a time with the customer agreeing to every aspect of the sale. The salesperson is always closing on each minor point and detail without the need to ask the final intimidating question most salespeople fear. Rather than being compelled to ask for the order, the salesperson and the customer agree to the sale.

This technique is effective because it recognizes the customer's needs and works to develop unique solutions. It constantly recognizes specific needs and reminds the customer that he or she is working together with the salesperson to meet them.

POINTS TO PONDER – SOMETHING TO THINK ABOUT

1. What has been your attitude toward closing? Is it an event or a process?
2. What are your typical closing techniques? How effective are they?

TRAINING ACTIVITY – APPLICATION & ACTION PLAN

1. Identify a major prospect or customer you are currently working on.
2. Physically plan the entire sales process from beginning to end as a decision tree.
3. Determine the key points or details for each step of the sale.
4. Plot the key points and details where you can close the customer to gain agreement on each point. Determine likely alternatives if agreement cannot be made on specific points or details.

5. Determine the potential points of the sale process where an agreement to buy is most likely to occur.
6. Plan a strategy for getting the customer to agree to each specific point.
7. When completed, put your plan into action.

4

Developing a Closing Strategy

Contrary to popular belief, closing is a strategy, not a singular event. Many salespeople follow outmoded sales formulas that conclude with the close. While salespeople may be successful with this approach, it is far from the most effective and efficient way to gain a customer's commitment to buy and continue to buy.

The business environment has undergone dramatic changes since the 1990s, and the way customers do business has changed as well. It only makes sense that salespeople change the way they sell their products.

IMPLICATIONS — WHAT THIS MEANS TO YOU

Customers are resistant to highly manipulative sales techniques that pressure them into a buying decision. Most buyers are more sophisticated than in the past, and many are highly educated in making productive purchasing decisions for their employers.

Most buyers want the salesperson to provide them with sufficient information to make an educated buying decision. They view the salesperson as a buying resource. Therefore, when salespeople attempt to use manipulative and outdated sales methods, they will meet with reluctance and skepticism.

Most salespeople who rely on outmoded methods fail to adequately analyze and identify the customer's needs, provide an adequate product solution and educate the customer about the value of their solution. They meet with the highest level of sales resistance, stalls and objections. Their failure to adequately prepare and educate the customer compels them to employ manipulative closing techniques.

This is important because salespeople who acutely recognize not only what customers want, but also how they buy, can craft an effective and successful closing strategy that assures they will meet with the least amount of resistance and the highest potential for success.

STRATEGIES, TIPS & TECHNIQUES TO APPLY

There are several factors that need to be considered in the development of an effective closing strategy, including:

Plan from the Onset of the Sale

The ultimate goal of every salesperson is to close the sale. To effectively do this, the salesperson must plan backward, beginning with the logical conclusion, which is the sale.

While this may appear to be time-intensive, there is no question that adequate preparation is required for a salesperson to be consistently successful.

Address All Customer Needs and Concerns

An effective closing strategy must identify all of the customer's needs and concerns and address these items with a carefully crafted product solution that the competition will find difficult to duplicate. This means the salesperson will factor in all of the unique features of his or her products and services and match these closely to the customer's needs.

Anticipate Potential Problems and Objections

Through careful planning and analysis, a salesperson should be able to anticipate and address any potential problems and objections before they are voiced. Often when potential problems are addressed up front and in a forthright manner, future problems and objections are minimized.

When problems and concerns are openly addressed before the customer is focused on them, they will be reluctant to look for further problems. They know the salesperson has taken the time to identify and address their concerns. This attention to detail builds and develops customer confidence.

Customer Agreement Should Be Paced

The salesperson should seek and obtain the customer's agreement on every detail and solution that occurs during the sales process. When a customer continually agrees to a series of minor issues, they will find it difficult to disagree when it's time to make a commitment to buy. The salesperson should take the time to review the points of agreement at the beginning and end of every customer contact. This works extremely well to reinforce the customer's commitment.

Arrive at a Logical Conclusion

An effective closing strategy should guide the customer into a predetermined series of steps and agreements that lead them to a logical conclusion: the commitment to buy. This can only be done when the salesperson takes the time to preplan their closing strategy.

Incorporate the Customer's Post-Sale Expectations

Salespeople should openly recognize the customer's post-sale fears that the product may not perform as promised or the salesperson may not be there to address any problems and/or concerns. An effective closing strategy should incorporate these fears as well as the customer's expectations. The salesperson should detail in writing what exactly will occur and when. This reference saves time, energy and frustration. It also works to build the customer's confidence that the salesperson will be there to meet their needs and concerns.

Recognize the Sale Does Not End with the Order

An effective closing strategy builds the customer's confidence. The salesperson should establish trust, assuring the customer that he or she will be there for the long-term and that the customer's needs and concerns are continually paramount.

POINTS TO PONDER — SOMETHING TO THINK ABOUT

1. How much planning do you use to determine the steps you need to lead a customer to a sale?
2. What steps do you go through to close a sale?

TRAINING ACTIVITY — APPLICATION & ACTION PLAN

1. Develop a template to use when planning a closing strategy for a new customer.
2. Detail all steps needed to lead the customer to the sale. Plan backwards from the sale.
3. Develop a decision tree that can be easily completed and followed that plans for all problems, objections, contingencies and variables.
4. Create a closing timeline that details the life of the sale and informs you of the steps you need to take and when.
5. Use this as a planning template for all new and existing sales.

5

Observing the Customer for Buying Signals

The most effective method of closing is to plan a closing strategy from the inception of the sale. It should be planned backward from the desired outcome—the sale. However, salespeople must still be observant of the customer's behavior as they implement their closing strategy.

Salespeople must be able to read between the lines and react to what is being said as well as what is not being said. Body language accounts for the majority of the communication in sales, and the customer may be sending distinct signals that the salesperson needs to be able to read and interpret. Properly done, the salesperson should be able to time their closing strategies based upon the buying signals the customer is sending.

IMPLICATIONS – WHAT THIS MEANS TO YOU

Salespeople who fail to develop exceptional listening skills will often miss obvious buying signals. Invariably these individuals are too busy pushing and pitching their product to take the time to step back and recognize what is happening.

Listening skills are an extremely high priority for successful salespeople. Salespeople must be able to quietly listen and observe the entire sales atmosphere to note what is happening and how the customer is reacting to their proposal. With time and patience, buying signals can become obvious if the salesperson takes the time to look for them.

The timing of the salesperson's closing strategies is vital to a successful outcome. If they are not attuned to the customer, they may move toward a commitment when the customer is displaying hesitant or negative buying signals. This is in direct conflict with the customer's state of mind, and is guaranteed to result in a stall or objection. Conversely, if the salesperson moves the customer toward a commitment at the time they are displaying positive buying signals, it will work to reinforce the customer's thinking and more often than not result in a positive outcome.

STRATEGIES, TIPS & TECHNIQUES TO APPLY

Customers can send a variety of buying signals that indicate the salesperson needs to take specific action to reinforce positive buying behaviors. Several of the most obvious buying signals include:

Hesitancy

The customer might display hesitancy as the salesperson is making his or her presentation. This behavior indicates the customer may be seeking out additional information to make a decision. At this point, they are considering the risk involved in buying from the salesperson.

When the salesperson observes this behavior, he or she immediately needs to reduce the customer's risk by providing additional information that puts him or her at ease. This can be done by the use of probing questions that explore the reasons for hesitancy. Once the salesperson has identified the reasons, he or she should be able to provide the information that makes their decision easier to make.

Indecision

Customers may display indecisive behaviors. This is quite different from a customer who is hesitant. These customers may need specific additional pertinent information including the order size, credit terms, delivery, back-end support and training to help them make a determination.

When the salesperson observes indecisive behavior, he or she needs to probe for the reasons behind the indecision and provide the necessary information to move the customer forward.

Reasoning Out Loud

Salespeople might experience a customer who is reasoning out loud. This indicates that the customer is selling him or herself on the sales proposal. Customers buy on emotion and justify their decision with the facts. When encountering this situation, salespeople should allow and encourage customers to reason out loud. They should minimize interrupting the customer's reasoning, but should support and reinforce their thinking and provide additional information on critical points.

Bargaining

When a customer begins to negotiate, this is a highly positive buying sign. The customer is attempting to obtain the best deal, testing the waters on various points until he or she arrives at the best possible terms.

Most often, customers don't realize they are sending signals to the salesperson. The salesperson should not indicate to the customer that they understand the signals he or she is sending. Rather, the salesperson should provide the necessary personal space the customer needs. Additionally, the salesperson should reassure the customer while providing information to support his or her buying decision.

POINTS TO PONDER — SOMETHING TO THINK ABOUT

1. What techniques do you use to observe customers' buying signals to move the sale forward? Explain.
2. Have you ever lost a sale by ignoring specific signals and signs the customer used? Explain what happened. What was the final result?

TRAINING ACTIVITY — APPLICATION & ACTION PLAN

Salespeople should identify the specific buying signals listed in this lesson that they have observed firsthand in their customers. They should pair up and use these examples to role-play situations that enable them to readily observe and develop statements to reinforce positive signals or overcome negative ones.

After each role-playing exercise, the salesperson in the role of the customer should explain to the other salesperson what actually happened and what cued him or her to the specific buying signal(s).

6

Managing Closing Objections

Many salespeople fail to understand how their customers buy. They fall short of gaining the customer's perspective and focus on the external process of selling. Because the sole objective is to get the sale, the salesperson sells too quickly. They arrive at the close long before the customer does and encounter a stream of objections as a result. The customer feels pressured and manipulated. The only recourse is to stall and voice objections to the sale.

IMPLICATIONS — WHAT THIS MEANS TO YOU

Over 80% of directly stated objections faced by salespeople are price/value objections. The customer is stating in one way or another that the product costs too much or that they cannot afford it. These objections are symptomatic of a larger problem: a low perceived value of the product or service being sold.

When salespeople encounter price/value objections early in the sale they can probe using history, symptom, cause, complication and cure questions. These questions work to help customers recognize the seriousness of their problem and increase the value of the solution.

By probing to overcome objections with questions, salespeople can head off the majority of objections and thereby avoid the necessity to address them later in the sales process.

STRATEGIES, TIPS & TECHNIQUES TO APPLY

If price/value objections occur late in the sales process, there are two typical causes triggering this concern: fear and a desire to get a better deal from the salesperson.

The first thing a salesperson must identify is what the underlying reason is for a late objection.

If a customer fear is identified as the cause of the objection, the salesperson must probe to draw the customer's fear out into the open.

Salespeople need to understand that fear is an emotional reaction. Buying decisions are emotional decisions justified with the facts. When fear is uncovered, the customer is second-guessing his or her decision or does not have sufficient facts to completely justify the decision.

Traditional objection-handling techniques are not an effective means of addressing customer fears. These techniques move too quickly toward a logical conclusion and do not get to the heart of the problem. Salespeople need to probe to uncover specific reasons behind the customer's fears and then openly discuss them. This allows the salesperson to calm the customer down and provide the additional information needed for the customer to justify his or her decision.

If the customer's objection is based upon a desire to get a better deal, the salesperson needs to sharpen their negotiating skills to bring the sale to a win-win agreement with the customer. The objective is to open the relationship rather than close the sale.

Since there are a small percentage of objections that fall outside of the price/value category, the salesperson can take a straightforward approach to handling these objections:

1. Ask the customer why they are voicing the objection. The question "why" allows the salesperson to find out the reasons behind the objection.
2. Verify the objection.
3. Empathize with the customer.

4. Offer a solution that has worked for a similar customer. Salespeople should have testimonials from a variety of customers to substantiate his or her claims.

Often these objections may have to do with the capabilities or capacity of the product or service. There may be a concern that the product or service being tendered is not an appropriate fit for the customer. These objections should come early on in the sales process. If they occur late in the process and do not involve the final details of the sale, it is a sign the salesperson has rushed the sale and has failed to provide sufficient data and information for the customer to justify their decision.

POINTS TO PONDER — SOMETHING TO THINK ABOUT

1. What are the typical types of objections you have encountered? Do 80% or more of the objections you encounter fall into the price/value category?
2. What steps do you personally take to minimize the occurrence of objections?

TRAINING ACTIVITY — APPLICATION & ACTION PLAN

1. Identify a customer you are currently working with to close the sale.
2. Clearly identify the customer's interests.
3. Determine the areas of agreement.
4. Identify the areas of disagreement that could result in an objection.
5. Create win-win solutions to resolve these differences before they occur.
6. Use the information and solutions you created to move the sales toward a successful conclusion.

7

The Customer's Expectations of Value

During the earlier stages of the sales process, customers develop a mental picture of the value of the results they expect to receive once they make the purchase. However, most customers have vague and undefined expectations of value. These intangible expectations lead to an uncertain perception of the ultimate value of the product or service. If the customer is not convinced that the solution he or she has purchased meets specific expectations, the salesperson will be unable to develop customer satisfaction.

IMPLICATIONS — WHAT THIS MEANS TO YOU

In addition to intangible and potentially unachievable expectations of the product's value, customers have high expectations of the salesperson: they want to see visible indications of the effort being expended on their behalf.

Many customers have felt the frustration of a salesperson making them feel important during the sale but quickly disappearing afterward. Salespeople reassure customers of their personal commitment to customer satisfaction during the sales process. The skeptical customer is just waiting to see whether the salesperson really does care or if they were simply manipulated into the sale.

For the dedicated salesperson who does in fact care about the customer and is honest about what they will receive, the challenge lies in thwarting and overcoming unethical competition. These individuals will inflate the customer's expectations and the level of service they promise to deliver. In many instances the dedicated salesperson loses out to the unethical competitor because of what they promise. The customer doesn't realize how empty the promises were until after the sale.

Salespeople are faced with a series of challenges in that many customers may be ignorant of the learning process of what a change in product or service entails. They may also lack familiarity with the changes that must be made to implement the solutions a new product provides. Finally, they may have undefined and unrealistic expectations as to the actual value of the product as well as the salesperson's involvement in post-sale activities. The long-term success of the customer relationship will depend on how the salesperson handles these challenges.

STRATEGIES, TIPS & TECHNIQUES TO APPLY

Throughout the closing of the sale, the salesperson must set realistic objectives and expectations. This is the foundation for sustainable customer satisfaction.

The salesperson is responsible for assuring that realistic, measurable objectives and expectations are set and agreed to by both the customer and the salesperson. The salesperson influences the development of these expectations and is present when they are created. This primary responsibility for customer satisfaction falls on the salesperson. This presents a tremendous opportunity to manage the customer's expectations and enhance the potential of creating complete satisfaction.

A primary cause of post-sale customer dissatisfaction is a lack of understanding by both customers and salespeople regarding the difference between needs and expectations. A need is something people require; an expectation is something individuals anticipate. The salesperson's objective is to eliminate surprises and disappointment. This is accomplished by defining the objectives and expectations clearly at the time the sale is closed and the order is signed.

When the salesperson identifies in specific terms what the customer can expect after the purchase, the customer is given a benchmark. This freezes his or her expectations, preventing them from rising, and gives the salesperson a goal to attain.

There are instances when value is difficult to measure. When this is the case, both the customer and the salesperson must agree on what factors will determine that value was delivered and how these factors should be measured.

The purpose of setting realistic objectives and expectations is to focus the customer on the value they expect to receive and how they will know when they receive it. This also provides the salesperson the ability to focus on the ways and means to attain the customer's expectations and deliver sustainable value.

If salespeople fail to identify realistic, attainable and measurable objectives and expectations, they are linking their success with a number of factors beyond their control. Performance indicators subject to influence by outside forces can also be used to unfairly judge the success of the sale. These uncontrollable forces can include the economy, government regulation, management decisions and practices.

POINTS TO PONDER — SOMETHING TO THINK ABOUT

1. Have you seen a customer relationship damaged because of undefined expectations?
2. Have you experienced problems because a customer was unable to define and measure the value of your product and service after a sale was made?

TRAINING ACTIVITY — APPLICATION & ACTION PLAN

1. Identify a prospect or customer that you are currently working to close.
2. During your next appointment, question the customer as to what his or her expectations are after the sale has been made.
3. Determine whether or not the customer's objective and expectations are realistic. If not, discuss them and make sure they are modified.
4. Discuss the criteria for the customer's acknowledging that the sale is a success and what will happen when the value he or she expects is received.
5. Determine how these specific objectives and expectations can be attained and how they will be measured.

8

Arriving at a Commitment

Even in the most congenial of sales relationships, the salesperson and the customer will need to conduct final negotiations before a commitment is secured. While there is no guarantee the customer will agree to the final proposal hammered out through negotiations, it is a positive sign that the customer is willing to invest the time and effort to work toward a mutual agreement.

IMPLICATIONS – WHAT THIS MEANS TO YOU

One of the pitfalls many salespeople encounter as they enter the final stages of closing and negotiating the sale is being able to specifically determine what they want from the customer. Often they are glad to get anything the customer has to offer. This places the salesperson at a distinct disadvantage since they have undermined their negotiating position even before it begins.

Salespeople must establish several negotiating positions for themselves before they meet with the customer. This provides them with the flexibility needed to successfully negotiate and close the sale. Three specific positions should be carefully considered.

- The target position – the position the salesperson is hoping to achieve
- The best-case position – the most favorable position in terms of products and profitability

- The worst-case position – the minimum amount the salesperson is prepared to accept

This is important to the salesperson because it establishes negotiating parameters to work within. Ideally, once negotiations begin, the salesperson has identified both the areas where concessions can be made and the positions he or she knows must be firmly maintained. If negotiations result in a position that is determined to be less than acceptable, then the salesperson knows it is time to walk away from a sale because it is not profitable or feasible for the company they represent.

STRATEGIES, TIPS & TECHNIQUES TO APPLY

Before entering into final negotiations, the salesperson needs to concentrate on the additional critical preparation of justifying each item of the proposal. This enables him or her to clarify whether the offer is reasonable.

Additionally, as price is often most customers' single focus, salespeople should generate a list of possible concessions other than price reduction. The salesperson should review the customer's needs and purchasing criteria that were developed throughout the sale. Examples of concessions that a salesperson can develop include: value-added services, additional options, training, customization, payment schedule and terms and conditions. As the salesperson prepares a list of possible concessions, he or she should place a dollar value next to each. This allows the salesperson to counter a customer's request for a price reduction with a concession that is of high value to the customer, but with a low cost to the salesperson's company.

Negotiations begin when the customer presents a demand. The natural reaction against a demand is to dig in, hold ground and fight. But to make the negotiating stance more productive, the salesperson should acknowledge and welcome the customer's demand, draw it in and destabilize the customer with the following strategies:

1. Paraphrase the demand to demonstrate to the customer that they were clearly heard and understood.
2. Ask the customer to present tangible reasons for the demand.

3. Get all additional demands on the table before making any concessions.
4. Seek a win-win solution that serves both parties' interests.
5. Avoid making immediate decisions. This can be done by probing the customer about different issues or deferring the decision to a higher authority. This should be done even if the salesperson has the personal authority to negotiate the agreement.

The key is for the salesperson to step back and allow the room to view the final agreement objectively and be able to realistically counter the customer's demands with appropriate concessions. This also allows the emotional negotiating environment to cool down so a workable agreement can be arrived at.

Once an agreement is reached, the salesperson should immediately confirm it in writing. This should include all of the specific details agreed to. Written confirmation avoids confusion and future misunderstandings that could undermine the relationship with the customer. If a contract is not immediately available, a memo of understanding should be used.

POINTS TO PONDER — SOMETHING TO THINK ABOUT

1. How have you approached final sales negotiations with your customers and prospects?
2. How much preparation do you undertake before you enter final sales negotiations?

TRAINING ACTIVITY — APPLICATION & ACTION PLAN

1. Identify a customer or prospect that you are near to closing.
2. Outline a range of negotiation positions including your target position, the best-case and worst-case position.

3. Develop a justification for each item listed in each position.
4. Generate a list of high-value concessions. Determine and note the dollar value of each of these.

About the Author

Timothy F. Bednarz, Ph.D. is CEO of the American Management Development Group, Inc. For over 20 years he has researched, designed and authored hundreds of learning and development programs used by Fortune 1000 companies.

He is also the author of *Great! What Makes Leaders Great. What They Did, How They Did It and What You Can Learn from It* (2011).

Speaking Availability

Timothy F. Bednarz, Ph.D. is available for speaking engagements for your next meeting or association event. He can be contacted at 800-654-4935 or by e-mail at timothy.bednarz@majorium.com.

Bulk Sales

Bulk sales of this book or any other titles available from Majorium Business Press. Inquiries can be directed to sales@majorium.com, or by phone at 800-6654-4935.

Quick Order Form

Fax orders: 715-342-1118. Send this form.

Telephone orders: Call 800-654-4935 toll-free. Have your credit card ready.

Email orders: sales@majorium.com

Postal orders: Majorium Business Press, 2025 Main Street, Stevens Point, WI 54481, USA.

Please send the following books:

____

____

____

____

Please send more FREE information on:

❑Catalog ❑Speaking/Seminars ❑Mailing Lists ❑Consulting

Name: ____________________________________

Address: __________________________________

City: ____________________ State: _____ Zip: ________

Telephone: ________________________________

Email address: _____________________________

Sales tax: Please add 5.5% for products shipped to Wisconsin addresses.

Shipping by air:

United States: $4.00 for first book and $2.00 for each additional product.

International: $9.00 for first book; $5.00 for each additional product (estimate).

Made in the USA
Monee, IL
23 June 2026

55592922R00026